GLORIA

Acknowledgements

My thanks to many people in RTÉ who have encouraged me in my career as a broadcaster, particularly my RTÉ lyric fm colleagues and *Gloria* production teams over the last twelve years.

To so many *Gloria* listeners around the world who have shown their appreciation.

To those who have helped me to produce such a beautiful book – to all those who read the text and made suggestions, to all at Hyperion Records and especially to my publishers, to Éamonn Hurley who first suggested the project and Anne Brady whose work on the art content has so wonderfully enriched it.

To my family – especially to my wife, Anne, to whom this book is dedicated.   *Tim Thurston*

A note on the Sacred Art included in this book

The task of choosing art from Irish collections to include in this book was enormous. In every corner of this island one can find Sacred Art, treasures which have been created – and continue to be created – by local and international artists.

Where possible, it was my intention to include a wide selection of work, over many periods, originating from different countries, in different media, yet all engaging in similar themes to the work of the composers in this book. With the help of many friends and advisors, I began choosing sacred stone carvings from the 9th century, and gradually began to include works created in wood, bronze, copper, silk, glass, linoleum, paper, vellum, linen, beeswax, oil, pencil and ink.

The final list of works is an entirely personal and eclectic collection. All those absent are merely works waiting patiently on my 'still to find' list.   *Anne Brady*

Title page image: *Angel with trumpet*, c. 1701, woodcut.
Image © The Board of Trinity College Dublin.

ASSOCIATED EDITIONS
www.associatededitions.ie

RTÉ lyric fm

GLORIA

AN INTRODUCTION TO 1000 YEARS
OF EUROPEAN SACRED MUSIC

TIM THURSTON

Æ

ASSOCIATED EDITIONS

CONTENTS

Opposite page: *Mother of God as Hodegetria* (showing the way) of the type called Kazanskya (Our Lady of Kazan). Image © Glenstal Abbey.

FOREWORD – THE STORY OF 'GLORIA'

Choral music has played a central role in my life from an early age. I have sung in choirs of many sorts for over fifty years and have been involved in running music festivals and writing and lecturing on a broad range of music. My broadcasting career began in the 1980s when I made a series on early music for Ireland's national broadcasting network RTÉ. In December 1996, the first prototype *Gloria*, of Christmas music, was broadcast on *Crosscurrents*, a programme featuring religious matters. After two series on RTÉ's then classical music channel, FM3 Music, the programme was one of the few to make the transition to the new Arts station, RTÉ lyric fm when it was launched in May 1999. *Gloria* has not missed a Sunday since.

I introduced the first series with these words…

I believe that the human voice is the most beautiful instrument of all and – especially unaccompanied – a choir can be the most moving of all musical sounds. The original purpose of most choral music was of course to enrich worship. However unless we are fortunate enough to be able to visit the very few cathedrals or churches which have managed to maintain the tradition of choral excellence, I am sad to say it rarely forms a part of contemporary liturgy. Neither does much of the music readily transfer to the concert hall. Luckily though there is a hugely rich treasury of recorded sacred music and in these programmes I'd like to share with you some of the very best which can be appreciated on so many different levels, by listeners of all faiths – and none.

Above and opposite page: details from the *Fagel Missal* (Delft, 1459–60), fol 160r. Images © The Board of Trinity College Dublin.

So, in those early days, my aim was simply to play the music – and let it speak for itself, to share with listeners the music I had loved all my life.

My experience running five Early Music Festivals had shown me that most music lovers who attended the many orchestral and chamber music concerts put on in Dublin were, in the main, unaware of the delights of early music. The wonderful sounds of Lassus, Dufay, Palestrina, Victoria, Machaut, Monteverdi, Schütz and Byrd were largely unknown to them. For many, their experience of 18th-century sacred music was often limited to the Passions of Bach and Messiahs performed by large forces at slow speeds – far from the dancing delights that we now know.

The structure of *Gloria* since the beginning has been chronological, starting with plainsong and working through the centuries, with Bach as the centre-piece, playing as much music pre-Bach as post. Especially in a programme which now runs for two hours, contrast is important – and not just in musical style. I try to vary the vocal and instrumental forces – with different types of choir – male and female voices only; boy trebles and sopranos on the top line; large choirs and small vocal ensembles with one voice to a part and choirs from all over the world. Solo voices are also featured.

Apart from the beauty of the music itself, the aspect of the programme which has been most appreciated is the manner in which it reflects the church year. This developed over the early months – it was obvious that Christmas music should be played at Christmas and that Lent should feature the wonderful penitential music written over the ages – Tenebrae Responsories, Reproaches and settings of Jeremiah's *Lamentations*. As I came across music setting texts for other Feasts – Advent, Epiphany, Candlemas, Pentecost, Trinity, Corpus Christi, St. Michael and All Angels, Marian Feasts and other Saints Days, I would programme them for the Sunday nearest to the feast.

When in 2005 the programme was extended to two hours, I began to feature the Cantatas of Johann Sebastian Bach – where feasible on the appropriate Sunday. This received much encouraging response. I have heard of no other radio station which has done this – surprising considering the supreme quality of the music and the scarcity of live performances. I rarely feature music outside the Christian tradition but often play Orthodox music and try to get a balance between the obviously Roman Catholic and Anglican traditions.

So, how have listeners responded over the years of the programme's existence? Considering the vast range of knowledge and musical experience of *Gloria* listeners, I am pleased to get as much positive reaction from people who are relative newcomers to serious music as from members of the music faculties of universities, and from staunch agnostics as from members of the clergy. Since the availability of the programmes on the web, I now get e-mails from around the world, many enquiries about the recordings and how to get hold of them; miraculous medals arrive, the occasional fundamentalist rant, and many touching expressions of gratitude from those for whom *Gloria* is a spiritual experience. I am also delighted to hear of music teachers who have told their students to tune in, particularly to learn of the glories of early music.

This book is in response to those who have expressed their pleasure at the music they hear on *Gloria* and wished for an overview of the story of Sacred Music in Western Europe. I have chosen twenty of the key composers and 'pen portraits' of each intersperse the story. After an opening track of chant, a composition by each of the twenty composers, all with an Advent or Christmas theme, is featured on the accompanying CD. The recordings come from the catalogue of the renowned independent UK recording company, Hyperion.

Sacred music and sacred art are inextricably intertwined and the images in this book –also on Advent and Christmas themes – are taken primarily from art in Irish collections.

Based on an article 'Musica Dei Donum Optimum' which first appeared in the Church of Ireland Journal 'Search' in Summer 2008.

INTRODUCTION

Calls distinguishable by their tonal properties were the earliest form of human communication – of warning, of greeting, of tribal belonging and, like the first cave paintings, of religious expression.

The making of music together is the most intense form of human co-operation requiring the highest degree of shared desires and understanding, of listening and working closely together. It is not surprising that its unifying properties have always been encouraged by church authorities and used as acts of worship from the earliest times and that choral singing remains today one of the best loved leisure activities throughout the world.

From the stories of Orpheus and his lyre and David and his harp, music has long been known as a powerful means of 'calming the soul' and scientific bases for its healing properties are now widely acknowledged.

In our own age of rationalism in western culture the arts have been relegated to areas regarded as decorative, enriching but not essential. In other societies, especially in the far east, the centrality of creative expression to human life and well-being is more fully integrated.

The transcendent, mystical, indeed ecstatic effect of music is by no means simply a religious view. Believers may describe music as a response to the pattern and order of God's creation but even an avowed agnostic, Ralph Vaughan Williams, described it as 'reaching out towards the utmost realities of ordered sound'.

Elizabeth Rivers, from *The Dove: a Christmas Sequence*, woodcut 1959, private collection. Image © Artist's Estate.

TIMELINE

COUNTRY	THE END OF THE AGE OF CHANT 1100	THE BEGINNINGS OF... 1150
GERMANY/AUSTRIA	HILDEGARD 1098–1179	
LOW COUNTRIES/FRANCE		LÉONIN c.1120–c.1200 PÉROTIN c.1160–c.1240
UNITED KINGDOM		
EAST EUROPE		

COUNTRY	RENAISSANCE POLYPHONY 1500	1550
GERMANY/AUSTRIA		HEINRICH SCHÜTZ 1585–1672 MICHAEL PRAETORIUS 1571–1621
LOW COUNTRIES/FRANCE	NICOLAS GOMBERT c.1495– c.1560 ORLANDO DI LASSO c.1532–1594	
SPAIN	TOMÁS LUIS DE VICTORIA c.1548–1611 CRISTÓBAL DE MORALES c.1500–1553 FRANCESCO GUERRERO 1528–1599	
ITALY	GIOVANNI P. DA PALESTRINA c.1525–1594 GIOVANNI GABRIELI c.1553–1612	CLAUDIO MONTEVERDI 1567–164.
UNITED KINGDOM	WILLIAM BYRD c.1539–1623 THOMAS TALLIS c.1505–1585 JOHN SHEPPARD c.1515–c.1559	ORLANDO GIBBONS 1583–1625
EAST EUROPE		

... AND THE FLOWERING OF RENAISSANCE POLYPHONY

300	1400	1450

| GUILLAUME DE MACHAUT 1300–1377 | **JOSQUIN DESPREZ** c.1449–1521
GUILLAUME DUFAY c.1400–1474
JOHANNES OCKEGHEM c.1410–1497 | JACOB OBRECHT c.1450–1505
HEINRICH ISAAC 1450–1517
PIERRE DE LA RUE c.1450–1518 |

| | JOHN DUNSTAPLE c.1380–1453 | JOHN TAVERNER c.1490–1545
ETON CHOIRBOOK
Late 15th Century |

E BAROQUE PERIOD

THE CLASSICAL AGE

00	1650	1750

| ETRICH BUXTEHUDE 1637–1707 | **JOHANN SEBASTIAN BACH** 1685–1750
GEORGE FRIDERIC HANDEL 1685–1759
JAN DISMAS ZELENKA 1679–1745
GEORG PHILIPP TELEMANN 1681–1767 | *continued overleaf* |

| AN–BAPTISTE LULLY 1632–1687
ARC-ANTOINE CHARPENTIER 1643–1704 | | |

| ACOMO CARISSIMI 1605–1674 | ANTONIO VIVALDI 1678–1741
ALESSANDRO SCARLATTI 1660–1725
DOMENICO SCARLATTI 1685–1757 | |

| | HENRY PURCELL 1659–1695 | |

Angel, Tim O'Neill, 1980, ink.
After a fifteenth century stone
carving in St. Nicholas
Church, Galway city.

COUNTRY	THE CLASSICAL AGE 1750	THE ROMANTIC MOVEME 1800
GERMANY/AUSTRIA	JOSEPH HAYDN 1732–1809 WOLFGANG AMADEUS MOZART 1756–1791 CARL PHILIPP EMANUEL BACH 1714–1788	FELIX MENDELSSOHN 1809–1847 ANTON BRUCKNER 1824–1896 FRANZ SCHUBERT 1797–1828 JOHANNES BRAHMS 1833–1897
LOW COUNTRIES/FRANCE		HECTOR BERLIOZ 1803–1869
ITALY	LUIGI CHERUBINI 1760–1842	GIUSEPPE VERDI 1813–1901
UNITED KINGDOM		
EAST EUROPE		

Stone carving of the
Flight into Egypt, 9th century,
a detail from the Moone High
Cross, Co. Kildare.
Photograph: Peter Harbison.

Lamb, Evie Hone, 1947, stained
glass window, by kind permission
of St. Francis Xavier's Church,
Gardiner Street, Dublin.
Photograph: Jozef Voda.
© Artist's Estate.

850	1900	1950
ABRIEL FAURÉ 1845–1890 AURICE DURUFLÉ 1902–1986	**FRANCIS POULENC** 1899–1963	OLIVIER MESSIAEN 1908–1992
ALPH VAUGHAN WILLIAMS 1872–1958	**SIR EDWARD ELGAR** 1857–1934 **BENJAMIN BRITTEN** 1913–1976 HERBERT HOWELLS 1892–1983	**JOHN TAVENER** *b.*1944 JOHN RUTTER *b.*1945 JAMES MACMILLAN *b.*1959
ERGEI RACHMANINOV 1873–1943	IGOR STRAVINSKY 1882–1971	**ARVO PÄRT** *b.* 1935

Angel blowing trumpet, Imogen Stuart,
973, bronze slide door handle,
t Michael's Church, Dun Laoghaire,
Co. Dublin. Photograph:
ohann Albrecht Cropp.
mage © Imogen Stuart.

THE FIRST MILLENNIUM – THE AGE OF CHANT

A s Christianity emerged from Judaism, so Christian chant grew principally out of the rich tradition of the Jewish cantor. The Old Testament is full of references to the honoured position of music in all human activities – and especially in worship. In the first millennium many different forms or 'rites' developed in many languages – Greek, Latin, Aramaic, Coptic and Hebrew – associated with the many sects and branches of Christianity within the two main divisions of the Churches of Rome and Byzantium following the great Schism of 1054.

In the Roman church five main rites arose and the Latin language began to predominate. The main shape of the liturgy, the eight monastic offices or hours of prayer surrounding the Mass, were first organised by St. Benedict (480–543). The texts of chants were mainly biblical, with the Psalms of David playing a central role. From New Testament times hymns were also used, freely composed in both text and music and sometimes in rhyme. St. Ambrose, the 4th-century Bishop of Milan, composed many which are still sung today and he encouraged this form of sacred worship.

It was only towards the end of the first millennium that the notation of chant began. Prior to this, the monks relied totally on memory. Considering the huge numbers of chants appropriate for every liturgy of every Sunday and Feastday, this was an astonishing feat. The chants, immediately recognisable to the faithful, remained central elements of sacred music as it unfolded through the centuries.

TRACK 1 – Gregorian Chant

Hodie Christus Natus Est – *Today Christ is born.*
This is one of the few chants that is still well known today. Benjamin Britten used it in his *Ceremony of Carols.*
The Choir of St. John's College, Cambridge – David Hill.

Opposite page: UNESCO World Heritage Site, *Skellig Michael*, Co. Kerry, a 7th-century monastic settlement. Photograph © Michael Diggin.

Book of Kells, c. 800,
'Virgin and child', fol 7v.
Image © The Board of Trinity College Dublin.

Stone carving of *Virgin and Child,* 9th century, a detail from
the Drumcliffe High Cross, Co. Sligo. Image © photographic
unit of the Department of Arts, Heritage and the Gaeltacht.

Hildegard of Bingen 1098–1179

Abbess Hildegard of Bingen holds a unique position in the history of music – no female composer has achieved such widespread fame – and no other named composer before the 14th century has as much surviving music. She included her seventy-seven songs, some as much as ten minutes long, in a volume entitled *Symphony of the Harmony of Celestial Revelations*. Her play *Ordo Virtutum*, is not only the first by a known composer but predates similar Morality Plays by over 100 years – and contains a further eighty-two melodies. Her music speaks over the centuries with remarkable dramatic force, freshness and eloquence. She was called 'The Sybil of the Rhine' and described herself as 'A Feather on the Breath of God'. One of the most versatile of all medieval figures – as poet, visionary, artist, healer, scientist and theologian – she founded two convents, corresponded with, and influenced, many of the key figures of her day. Some 300 letters survive written to no fewer than four Popes, King Henry II of England, St. Bernard of Clairvaux, Emperor Frederick Barbarossa, whom she met, Peter Abelard and numerous other lay and spiritual leaders. Hildegard firmly spoke her mind on both theological matters and on the complex and turbulent world of the ecclesiastical politics of the day. Her music and writings have become popular with, among others, feminist theologians and ecologists.

TRACK 2 – Hildegard of Bingen

O Viridissima Virga – *Hail, O greenest branch, sprung forth in the airy breezes of the prayers of the Saints.* This chant is sung by male voices, accompanied by the string drone of a symphony, a medieval predecessor of the hurdy-gurdy. The text celebrates Mary as a branch of the Tree of Jesse.
Gothic Voices – Christopher Page.

THE FLOWERING OF RENAISSANCE POLYPHONY

The turn of the millennium saw musicians begin to experiment with two or more independent musical lines. This developed quickly, greatly aided by notation, which allowed for ever more complex compositions. The great Gothic Cathedral of Nôtre-Dame in Paris was the first centre of these initial steps of polyphony, and compositions by Léonin and Pérotin preserved in the 12th-century *Magnus Liber Organi* are the best known surviving works of the Nôtre-Dame School.

Léonin (Magister Leoninus) *c.*1120–*c.*1200

What little we know of the exciting early developments of polyphony of 12th-century Paris comes from a treatise by an English monk, possibly from Bury St. Edmunds, who is known as Anonymous IV. He tells how, around 1170, Léonin composed a cycle of two part music based on the chants for the principal feasts of the church year, the *Magnus Liber Organi* – the great book of organum. Organum comprised a lower voice singing long, sometimes drone-like notes, often based on the original plainchant melody, while the upper voice provides a more decorated and faster-moving line. A generation later, Pérotin, the other name mentioned by Anonymous IV, both modified the original two part music and added compositions of three and four parts. There is considerable uncertainty about dates, the roles of these figures in the Cathedral of Nôtre-Dame and the method of performance, especially in its rhythm, but these works were the first steps away from the purity of chant towards polyphony.

TRACK 3 – Léonin

Gloria from ***Advent Responsory*** – *Glory be to the Father and to the Son and to the Holy Ghost.*
This is the doxology at the end of the Responsory: 'Judea and Jerusalem, fear not; tomorrow ye shall go forth and the Lord shall be with you'. After the two voices sing the Gloria, the Schola chants a repeat of the respond.
Red Byrd, Yorvox.

Flemish Illuminated miniature of the *Nativity* (detail), *c.* 1250.
Image © the Chester Beatty Library, CBL W 061, f.8v.

Angel blowing a trumpet, *c.* 13th century, stained glass. This panel
comes originally from the former Augustinian abbey of Bristol,
now Bristol Cathedral. Image © The Hunt Museum.

By the end of the 13th century, as well as a vast number of motets of many sorts, polyphonic settings of the Ordinary of the Mass were being made. The earliest by a named composer is the *Messe de Nostre-Dame* from around 1364 by Guillaume de Machaut. The harmonic language of early polyphony, even up to Machaut's Mass, sounds strange to our ears. It was the music of English composer John Dunstaple and the Masters of the Franco-Flemish School: Guillaume Dufay, Johannes Ockeghem, Jacob Obrecht and above all Josquin Desprez, influenced by a great growth in the academic study of musical theory, which led to chants being ornamented by weaving lines of counter melodies and a harmonic language which laid the foundation of western classical music.

In England, the 15th century was dominated by rich and florid music in many parts, such as those included in the Eton Choirbook – copied for use in Eton College where it is still held – and in the sacred works of John Taverner. Thomas Tallis and William Byrd were the key figures of Elizabethan times, composing music for the Catholic rite and for the services of the new Anglican church.

In the 15th and 16th centuries the Low Countries and northern France produced an amazing number of composers and singers. Most Italian chapel choirs could boast a Flemish bass in their ranks and these musicians sowed the seeds for the great musical developments which were to come from Italy.

The principal composers of the Spanish Renaissance, Cristóbal de Morales, Francisco Guerrero and Tomás Luis de Victoria all studied in Rome. Their music is passionate and dramatic with many Lamentations, and Passion music for Holy Week. From the early 16th century, both Spanish and Portuguese colonists brought musicians to the New World, and a rich tradition of liturgical music with Native American influences grew up in many cities of Central and South America.

Throughout Europe, Renaissance composers held positions in both chapel and court and were often fine singers and instrumentalists, writing music in many genres. Both Machaut and Dufay took the tradition of the Troubadours further, composing love songs of the greatest beauty.

In spite of a Papal Bull forbidding the use of such songs as the *cantus firmus* for Mass settings and motets, this practice became very popular, together with long phrases which made the words indistinguishable. There was a loosening of the influence of chant and Masses were often composed freely, without any reference to previous music, chant or otherwise. The Catholic Counter Reformation sought to purify such settings, banning the use of instruments and insisting on the clarity of the text.

Josquin Desprez *c.*1449–1521

Although he is considered the central figure of the Franco-Flemish School, the life of Josquin Desprez is poorly documented and his exact date and place of birth unknown. Like so many musicians from the Low Countries he crossed the Alps and served the Sforza family in Milan. He was the highest paid singer in the history of Milan Cathedral. He sang in the Sistine Chapel choir from 1486 – recent restoration uncovered the letters 'JOSQUINJ' carved into the Chapel wall – and a portrait of him is attributed to Leonardo da Vinci. He served the Este court in Ferrara and around 1503 returned to his home region, Condé, near Lille, where he died in 1521. His works were regarded as models by many theorists and composers and his fame spread widely thanks to many publications by the early printers – Petrucci in Venice and Attaignant in Paris. His name was so renowned that after his death many anonymous compositions were attributed to him, although recent scholarship has reduced his authenticated output, long thought to be about twenty Masses, 100 motets and 75 secular works. Many of his *Chansons* were hugely popular and provided the basis for instrumental variations. He was the favourite composer of Martin Luther and Rabelais and his pre-eminence was unchallenged until Palestrina's time.

Fagel Missal (Delft, 1459–60), 'Adoration of Magi', fol 24v.
Image © The Board of Trinity College Dublin.

The *Nativity Scene* from the Waterford Magi Cope, second half of the fifteenth century. Image © Waterford Museum of Treasures at the Choristers' Hall, Museum of Medieval Waterford.

Inter Natos Mulierum *– Among them that are born of women there hath not risen a greater than John the Baptist.*

This rich five-part motet sets two verses concerning John the Baptist from the Gospels of Matthew and John. Josquin's authorship is in doubt though it is ascribed to him in two of the three known sources.

The Binchois Consort – Andrew Kirkman.

Giovanni Pierluigi da Palestrina *c.*1525–1594

 Named after his birthplace to the east of Rome, he sang as a boy in S. Maria Maggiore in Rome in 1537. After seven years as a singer and organist back in Palestrina, he moved to Rome at the age of twenty-six where he worked in some of the most prestigious churches in the city, including the Sistine Chapel, until his death in his seventieth year. The widespread publication of his sacred works brought him the reputation as the first great Italian composer. In 1577 he was asked to edit the Church's chant books according to the Council of Trent's guidelines for a greater musical simplicity and clarity of text, and his *Missa Papae Marcelli* reputedly persuaded the Council of Trent against more stringent restrictions in the use of polyphony. His 104 mass settings and over 300 motets have a seamless, restrained perfection with all voices in balance and, unlike most composers of Renaissance and Baroque times, his music has enriched Catholic worship ever since. Bach arranged his *Missa Sine Nomine* and many composers of the 18th and 19th centuries made a particular study of his music.

Kyrie from ***Missa Hodie Christus Natus Est*** *– Lord, have mercy, Christ, have mercy, Lord, have mercy.*

In Palestrina's third book of motets, published in Venice in 1575, was an eight part *Hodie Christus Natus Est* based on the Christmas Antiphon and this joyous Mass uses musical material from the motet.

Westminster Cathedral Choir – Martin Baker.

William Byrd *c.*1539–1623

William Byrd is regarded as the greatest composer of England's Golden Age, writing in most musical genres of the time. Even during his lifetime he was dubbed 'A Father of British Musicke'. His date, and place, of birth are uncertain but he grew up in London and was a pupil of Thomas Tallis. His first recorded position was as organist and choirmaster of Lincoln Cathedral, at the age of nineteen. In 1572 he became a Gentleman of the Chapel Royal and organist, jointly with Tallis. This began his contact with the Court and, in 1575, Queen Elizabeth I granted both composers a monopoly on the printing and selling of part-music and manuscript paper. It was the respect that she held for them as musicians which enabled them to continue composing Catholic music. Although Byrd's Services and Anthems for the Anglican Church were as fine as any, it was his three Masses, Mass Propers and Latin motets which are his towering achievements. He remained a Catholic all his life, retiring from the Chapel Royal to spend the last third of his life living in rural Essex, where he died in his eighties. His large output of keyboard works was unparalleled and he also left many consort songs and other pieces of vocal and instrumental music.

TRACK 6 – Byrd

Tollite Portas / Ave Maria – *Lift up your gates, ye Princes, and the King of Glory will come in / Hail Mary, full of grace.*
From the first of two books titled *Gradualia* of 109 motets, published in 1602, this five-part Gradual with its connected *Ave Maria* sets verses from Psalm 23 for Lady Mass during the season of Advent.
Westminster Cathedral Choir – Martin Baker.

The Virgin and Child Enthroned, with Saints John the Baptist and Lucy, Marco Palmezzano, *c*.1460–1539, Italian, 16th century, 1513, tempera and oil on wood panel, unframed: 218 x 188 cm. Photo © National Gallery of Ireland, NGI 117.

The Flight into Egypt, Jan de Beer, *c.*1475–1528. Flemish, 16th century, oil on oak panel, unframed: 33.5 x 23.7 cm. Photo © National Gallery of Ireland, NGI 1001.

Albrecht Dürer (1471–1528), *Adoration of the Magi*. Woodcut from *The Life of the Virgin, c.* 1511. Image © the Chester Beatty Library, CBL Wep 69.

Virgin and Child (detail), Rosarium of Phillip II of Spain, Simon Bening, c. 1530, Flemish. Image © the Chester Beatty Library, CBL W 99, f.44v.

Tomás Luis de Victoria 1548–1611

Tomás Luis de Victoria was Spain's most renowned composer and a central figure of Renaissance music. He was born in Avila and showed such musical promise as a boy singing in the Cathedral that he was sent to the German Jesuit College in Rome when his voice broke. During his twenty years there he was ordained and worked with Europe's musical elite including, it is almost certain, Palestrina. He served a number of churches and became Maestro di Cappella of the German College. He became famous through his sumptuously published collections of motets and Masses but returned to Spain in 1580 to serve as Chaplain to King Philip II's sister, the Empress Maria, at the Convent of St. Clare in Madrid. He made a further visit to Rome to supervise the printing of his works and attended Palestrina's funeral in 1594. All his compositions were of sacred choral music – around twenty masses and fifty motets, eighteen Magnificats and some superb music for Holy Week, in which his intense mystical fervour and dramatic word-painting are particularly telling. His masterpiece is his final work – a Requiem written for the Empress and published in 1605.

TRACK 7 – Victoria

O Magnum Mysterium *– O great mystery and wondrous thing that the animals beheld the new-born King lying in a manger.*

This charming text has appealed to composers through the ages. It is from the Responsory for Christmas Matins and this setting in four parts published in 1572, with its dancing 'Alleluia', is one of Victoria's most popular motets.

Westminster Cathedral Choir – David Hill.

THE BAROQUE PERIOD

The term 'Baroque' comes from a Portuguese word meaning 'a pearl of irregular shape'. It was applied first in France to the world of art to describe anything strange, irregular, unusual or extravagant. It was later applied to the style of European music from around 1600 to 1750.

During the late 16th century, Italy saw the beginnings of major developments in all forms of musical composition. The Church was no longer the focal point of such changes and developments in printing allowed for the widespread circulation of music. The new instrumental styles, the growing popularity of melodic solo rather than choral singing, the greater use of contrast and expression of emotion, and the use of Basso Continuo were slowly incorporated into sacred music.

The Basilica of St. Mark's in Venice was a key centre – Claudio Monteverdi used its golden spaces to contrast different musical forces, instrumental and choral, and composed florid motets and Psalm settings using the full array of baroque styles, including those from the world of opera.

Rome saw the early development of the cantata, both sacred and secular. The characteristics of this genre included a number of contrasting movements with solo voices predominating, a growing use of recitative, and a type of vocal writing from the operatic world where the voice follows the natural rhythms and accentuation of speech. The principal figures were Giacomo Carissimi and Alessandro Scarlatti.

Music was an important component in the success of the Reformation in Northern Europe but it was to Italy that aspiring young German musicians came to learn the latest trends. Heinrich Schütz spent two periods in Venice and left a rich output of sacred music, incorporating the Italianate sparkle, imaginative word-painting and the use of dissonance, with his more serious Lutheran expression. Throughout Reformation Europe there was a move towards settings of vernacular texts.

The Italian composer, Jean-Baptiste Lully, created for King Louis XIV a flowering musical life in Paris, incorporating the best of Italian and French styles. The main emphasis was on dazzling and majestic royal entertainments with opera, theatre and dance, but French Baroque composers also brought their particularly fresh dancing spirit to Church music.

After the Puritans' destruction of so much of the country's Christian fabric and tradition during the Commonwealth, Henry Purcell stands out in England, putting his individual stamp on to Italian innovations – and those French musical ideas that King Charles II had experienced at the court of Louis XIV and was determined to match.

The year 1685 saw the birth of three great names in music. Domenico Scarlatti's main output was 555 harpsichord sonatas; George Frideric Handel's operas, oratorios and orchestral music are his most renowned legacy, though both wrote some fine sacred music; and Handel composed the most popular sacred work of all, *Messiah*. Johann Sebastian Bach considered all of his music to be sacred – he wrote 'SDG', 'Soli Deo Gloria – Glory to God alone', even on his instrumental music. His *Passions, B Minor Mass* and around 200 surviving cantatas stand as the greatest outpouring of music in praise of God – and the cantatas as the greatest corpus of unfamiliar masterpieces. No family could better illustrate the strength of the musical gene. Of the eighty-five male members of the Bach family from 1550–1850, seventy earned their livelihoods through music – and fifty-two of those were called Johann!

Claudio Monteverdi 1567–1643

Claudio Monteverdi was one of the major innovators in the history of music, composing the earliest great opera, *Orfeo* in 1607, eight books of madrigals published over a period of nearly fifty years which show an astonishing compositional development, and what is widely considered the first great masterpiece in music, the *Vespro della Beata Vergine*, the 1610

Vespers. He was born in Cremona and published both motets and madrigals in his early twenties. In 1591 he moved to Mantua to serve the Gonzaga family and in 1613 became Maestro di Cappella at St. Mark's in Venice. His Mass settings are monuments to the Franco-Flemish school, but the 1610 Vespers and the forty works he published in *Selva Morale e Spirituale* in 1641 at the end of his life include bold, experimental and virtuoso music for voices and instruments, representing the pinnacle of the early Baroque period. He also composed a number of operas for the new opera houses of Venice.

TRACK 8 – Monteverdi

Christe Redemptor Omnium *– O Christ, Redeemer of all men.*
Monteverdi sets this Office Hymn for Christmas Vespers for three male voices and two violins. Compared to his dramatic Psalms, it is relatively simple in form, with a series of rising phrases and ornamentation from both voices and instruments.
The Choir of the King's Consort – Robert King.

Heinrich Schütz 1585–1672

Impressed by his early musical promise, Landgrave Moritz of Hesse brought Heinrich Schütz to sing as a boy in his court at Kassel in central Germany and then, in 1609, persuaded him to leave his law studies at Marburg University to go to Venice to develop his musical skills with Giovanni Gabrieli. After periods back at Kassel and Dresden, he was given leave of absence to return to Venice for further studies, most likely with Monteverdi. His first publication from his mid twenties was of nineteen Italian madrigals, but apart from a lost opera, *Dafne*, from 1627, all his large output thereafter was of sacred music. He was the most internationally renowned German composer before Bach and his music brings together the serious Lutheran approach with a dramatic colour from the influence of Venice. Dresden remained his musical base but the Thirty Years War had a disastrous effect on life there.

Three angels in a landscape, c. 1595, India.
Image © the Chester Beatty Library, CBL In 62.2.

Saint Joseph with the Christ Child, Guercino, 1591–1666.
Italian, 17th century, *c*.1637, oil on canvas, unframed:
99 x 77 cm. Photo © National Gallery of Ireland, NGI 192.

The Infant Saint John Playing with a Lamb, Bartolomé Estebán Murillo, 1617–1682, Spanish, 17th century, 1670–1680. Oil on canvas, Unframed: 61 x 44 cm.
Photo © National Gallery of Ireland, NGI 33.

Armenian illuminated miniature of the *Adoration of the Magi* (detail), 17th century.
Image © the Chester Beatty Library, CBL Arm 605, f.46v.

Schütz then travelled to other German cities in search of work and also spent periods serving the Danish Court. He composed Psalm settings in the polychoral Venetian style and although he left no specifically instrumental works, instruments played a major part in many of his later motets. Towards the end of his long life, he wrote three dramatic Passion settings with the Gospel narrated by an Evangelist with polyphonic passages for other characters and crowd scenes.

TRACK 9 – Schütz

From *The Christmas Story*
The Evangelist tells of the Heavenly Host, they sing 'Glory to God' and the Shepherds, with recorders, hasten to Bethlehem.
The King's Consort – Robert King.

Johann Sebastian Bach 1685–1750

For three centuries in Central Germany, the Bach family represented an astonishing concentration of musical talent, and the compositions of the towering figure of Johann Sebastian have had as great an influence as any on the musical world ever since. Apart from opera, every other form of Baroque musical expression was brought to its pinnacle in Bach's music which, after a century of comparative neglect after his death, is now widely revered and respected. Son of Johann Ambrosius, a town musician in Eisenach, Sebastian was orphaned at the age of ten and went to live with his elder brother. Aged fifteen, he won a scholarship to St. Michael's School in Lüneburg. There he sang in the choir and continued his musical education. After various musical jobs in Weimar, Arnstadt and Mühlhausen he worked for nine years as organist and chamber musician to the Duke of Saxe-Weimar. In 1717 he left Weimar for Cöthen, where the Duke had a musical court. In 1723 Bach gained the prestigious post of Thomaskantor and Director Musices at Leipzig where he remained for the rest of his life. Although the city had no permanent opera house, it was a thriving musical centre in every other respect and Sebastian contributed with prodigious amounts of musical compositions. The quality of his keyboard works, especially for organ, is supreme and his 300 or so church Cantatas – a third of which have not survived – represent an unsurpassed legacy. The two surviving *Passions* of St. John and St. Matthew and the *B Minor Mass* remain among the most popular and moving sacred musical expressions and pay witness to his deep Lutheran faith. He rejoiced in celebrating life with his large family, and often had strained relations with his employers. Death was an ever-present reality throughout his life. He had twenty children, but buried ten of them in infancy. Diabetes and complications following two eye operations hastened his own death.

TRACK 10 A — Bach

In Dulci Jubilo – *In Sweet Jubilation:* Organ Chorale Prelude BWV729
This 14th-century German hymn is one of the best loved Christmas tunes and has been used by many composers. Bach's *Chorale Prelude* composed in the 1730s in Leipzig is frequently chosen by organists as part of Christmas celebrations. Christopher Herrick on the Metzler organ of the Stadtkirche, Zofingen in Switzerland.

TRACK 10 B — Bach

Wie Schön Leuchtet Der Morgenstern – *How Brightly Shines the Morning Star*
Chorale from Cantata BWV1. Bach used this popular chorale a number of times in both choral and organ works. The cantata is for the Feast of the Annunciation but the chorale is often played during Christmastide. The second horn flourishes joyously. The King's Consort – Robert King.

George Frideric Handel 1685–1759

After some time as organist in the cathedral of his birthplace, Halle, near Leipzig and playing the violin and harpsichord in the Opera House in Hamburg, Handel spent three formative years in the main musical cities of Italy, Rome, Venice, Florence and Naples. In Rome he composed music for Vespers for the Carmelites and some Italian Cantatas. He spent a short period as Kapellmeister to the Elector

Interior of the Music Hall, Fishamble Street, Dublin, where the first performance of Handel's *Messiah* was given on 13 April 1742 at 12 noon. Image from *Walker's Hibernian Magazine*, March 1794 (Joly 05), courtesy of the National Library of Ireland.

of Hanover before he began visiting London to direct his operas. He moved there permanently in 1712, becoming a central figure in its musical life, first with a series of dramatic Italian operas and then, due to changing fashions and rival opera houses, with oratorios in English, mainly from biblical or classical sources. He wrote two sets of Anthems, seventeen for the Duke of Chandos and four for the Coronation of King George II in 1727. In 1742, in Dublin, he directed the first performance of *Messiah*, which remains the most popular of all choral works. His output of fine instrumental music, Organ Concertos, Concerti Grossi, *The Water Music*, sonatas and keyboard works help to place him, with Bach, as the supreme composer of the Baroque era.

TRACK 11 – Handel

For Unto Us A Child Is Born – from *Messiah*
In just three weeks Handel composed the music setting to Charles Jennens' selection of biblical verses telling the story of Christ. This chorus is a high-point of part one of the work.
Polyphony – Stephen Layton.

A priest worships an image of the Virgin and Child in a shrine, c. 1800,
Lucknow, India. Image © the Chester Beatty Library, CBL In 63.18.

THE CLASSICAL AGE

In 18th-century Europe the spirit of the Enlightenment encouraged freedom in every aspect of life and thought, and there was a further loosening in the influence of church and monarchy. Yet the two great composers of 18th-century Masses, Mozart and Haydn, both relied on such patronage. Salzburg Cathedral for Mozart and the Esterhazy family for Haydn. The emerging symphonic style of the classical orchestra was a central feature of the Masses of both composers. It was in Vienna that Schubert wrote his six Masses – very much in the tradition of Haydn, and Beethoven his two Mass settings as well as the epitome of a musical statement of the Enlightenment spirit; his *9th (Choral) Symphony*. Many such 18th-century choral compositions were composed for the concert hall rather than for liturgical use.

Although England produced no major composers in the 18th or 19th centuries, domestic music making and concert going thrived with Haydn and many other composers making frequent visits. The popularity of the oratorio, especially those by Handel, and the growth of the congregational hymn were the main influences during the 18th century. The spread of Non-Conformist churches was greatly helped by the power of communal singing. Charles Wesley, whose brother John founded Methodism, composed over 6000 hymns.

Joseph Haydn 1732–1809

At the age of six, Joseph Haydn left his impoverished family in Rohrau in Austria, near the Hungarian border, to begin his musical studies, singing as a boy in the choir of St. Stephen's Cathedral in Vienna until he was eighteen. After precarious years as a freelance musician, playing the violin and keyboard instruments, teaching and accompanying, in 1761 he began his long service to the Esterhazy family. He composed in every genre of music and his 108 symphonies earned him the title of 'The

Father of the Symphony. He deserves a similar accolade for writing more than sixty string quartets and wrote twice that number of trios. His oratorios, *The Seasons* and *The Creation*, are still very popular today, though his operas never gained any great success. His employers allowed him time to travel and he became internationally renowned, being especially popular in London. He was required to compose Masses for the Nameday of Princess Maria Esterhazy and the six written between 1796 and 1802 are among his finest works. He and his younger brother Michael, also a composer, were close friends of Mozart, and Beethoven took lessons from him. His joyous music belies an unhappy personal life, though his Catholic faith remained strong.

TRACK 12 – Haydn

Et Incarnatus Est *– And was incarnate by the Holy Ghost –* from *Missa Solemnis.*
This Mass, also called *Harmoniemesse,* was Haydn's last major work composed in 1802 when he was seventy. This is the central part of the Credo with the soprano voice and clarinet prominent.
Lynda Russell – soprano, The Brandenburg Orchestra – David Hill.

Wolfgang Amadeus Mozart 1756–1791

In his short life – he died aged thirty-five – Wolfgang Amadeus Mozart composed over 600 works and developed many musical forms – the piano concerto, opera, the piano sonata and the symphony – to their highest classical expression. A child prodigy, his father Leopold took him aged seven, and his sister Nannerl, on a tour of European courts, playing to the English and French royal families. Further trips away from their home in Salzburg took them to Vienna, Munich and Italy, the young Mozart composing constantly. From the age of eighteen he worked, intermittently and unhappily, as Konzertmeister at the Court of the Prince-Archbishop of Salzburg, but failed to find any better position on his many further trips. In 1781 he was dismissed and spent the rest of his life in Vienna as a freelance teacher, publisher and performer. He composed to commission but opera remained the centre of his attention. He achieved some fame and for a time lived lavishly, though he died in poverty.

During his time at Salzburg he composed sixteen Mass settings, litanies, music for Vespers, sacred songs, motets, and instrumental music to be performed during the Mass. Many of the Masses were short, in the form known as 'Missa Brevis'. The *Great C Minor Mass* of 1783 is however one of his finest works and in the last year of his life he wrote his two most renowned sacred works, the motet, *Ave Verum Corpus* and his unfinished *Requiem*.

TRACK 13 − Mozart

Epistle Sonata In F Major, K244

Usually Mozart would have improvised on the organ after the reading of the Epistle during the Gospel procession but, on special occasions, a short composition was called for and seventeen such works have survived. This charming work features the organ.

Ian Watson − organ, The King's Consort − Robert King.

THE ROMANTIC MOVEMENT

The political upheavals of the early 19th century led to the tension between hope and despair which became a central thrust of the Romantic movement. Opportunities came to composers through the popularity of domestic music making, the wide availability of printed music and the development of public concert halls. Some composers, like Berlioz and Liszt, were forward-looking and others more influenced by the past like the Lutherans Mendelssohn and later Brahms, both of whom composed sacred music throughout their lives. Bruckner forged his own path, a devout Catholic and professional church musician for most of his career.

In 1833, a Benedictine Community was founded in Solesmes near Le Mans and began a movement to restore Gregorian Chant. After the Revolution in France developments in music for the organ predominated, although Fauré's *Requiem* of 1888 was, and remains, highly popular.

From the late 18th century, there were exchanges between Russian and Italian musicians. It was not until 100 years later that Tchaikovsky and Rachmaninov were influenced by the richness of the music of the Orthodox Church in their large choral works, though these were not liturgical. The Russian Revolution forced the Church underground – and many composers into exile. The European Nationalist movements were given some sacred expression – particularly from the Czech, Dvořák and Grieg in Norway.

Felix Mendelssohn Bartholdy 1809–1847

Like Mozart, Felix Mendelssohn was a child prodigy and died in his thirties. His father, a cultured Jewish Berlin banker, converted to Lutheranism and added the name Bartholdy. After concert tours of England, Scotland, Italy and France, he spent a year in Düsseldorf where he conducted many of the works of Handel and, at the age of twenty, directed a performance of Bach's *St. Matthew Passion*, sparking a revival of interest in Bach's music. In his ten years in Leipzig he was involved in every aspect of the city's musical life as conductor, concert organiser and founder and director of the Leipzig Conservatory. He was particularly popular in England, especially for his two great Oratorios, *Elijah* and *St. Paul* and he premiered many of his compositions during his ten visits there. He wrote organ and choral music – both Psalm settings and anthems – throughout his life, including the most famous solo for the boy treble voice, *O for the Wings of a Dove*. His *Violin Concerto* from 1844 epitomises the Romantic in music.

From **Six Anthems for the Different Times of the Year** for eight-part choir.
In 1843 Mendelssohn became director of the Berlin Cathedral Choir for whom
these short works were composed. For Advent, **Lasset uns Frohlocken** – *Let us be
cheerful, the Saviour is near* – for Christmas, **Frohlocket** – *Rejoice , O ye people on
Earth* and for New Year's Day, **Herr Gott, du bist unsre Zuflucht** – *Dear God, you are
our refuge.*
The Corydon Singers – Matthew Best.

Anton Bruckner 1824–1896

 On the death of his father, a village organist
and schoolmaster, the thirteen-year old Anton
Bruckner was sent to study music at the renowned
St. Florian Monastery in Linz. In 1855 he became
the organist at Linz Cathedral and then moved
to Vienna where he held various teaching posts.
Most of his time was spent touring as an organ
recitalist and composing ten symphonies of
considerable grandeur and complexity, with
Beethoven and Wagner as the main musical influences. His many
sacred choral works express his devout faith in a much more intense
way. After considerable early set-backs he achieved fame through the
symphonies, although he was an exceedingly modest and simple man,
prone to depression. He died aged seventy-two and is buried beneath
his favourite organ in St. Florian's Monastery.

TRACK 15 — Bruckner

Virga Jesse Floruit – *Now hath blossomed Jesse's rod, a Virgin bears
both man and God.*
This Christmas motet from 1885 is full of drama and rich romantic
harmonies with a joyous Alleluia. Polyphony – Stephen Layton.

The Dawn of Christianity (*The Flight into Egypt*),
Joseph Mallord William Turner, 1841,
© National Museums Northern Ireland Collection
Ulster Museum, BELUM.U224

THE TWENTIETH CENTURY

The nationalist spirit continued with Kodály in Hungary, Janáček in Bohemia and Penderecki in Poland. Igor Stravinsky was influenced both by his Orthodox roots and the music of Baroque and Renaissance times and composed some sacred works in his own unique style. Since the advent of perestroika, recordings of Russian choirs singing Russian Orthodox music have made a considerable impact – especially with their phenomenal basses.

After two centuries of musical mediocrity the final years of the 19th century saw a renaissance of music in England through Hubert Parry and the Irishman, Charles Villiers Stanford. Their church music is still sung throughout the Anglican world. In spite of ambivalent relationships with the Church, Elgar, Vaughan Williams, Holst, Britten and Tippett all composed fine sacred choral works, much of their music looking back to the richness of earlier times.

In recent years John Rutter's tuneful sacred music contrasts with the deep spiritual influence of the music of John Tavener and the Scot, James MacMillan, who has led a move towards more liturgical music being written by a younger generation of British composers. Tavener, along with Henryk Górecki from Poland and Estonian Arvo Pärt, have been termed 'The Holy Minimalists', many of their compositions being of a slow meditative nature with limited melodic or rhythmic development.

The revival of interest in early music has had a strong influence on choral singing – particularly in the reduction of choral vibrato and hence a greatly improved intonation. This is in contrast with Italian choirs where the style of most choral singing still aspires to that of the opera house.

Three French composers stand out – Maurice Duruflé whose 1947 *Requiem* has become as popular as Fauré's and Francis Poulenc, a particularly individual voice. Although Olivier Messiaen composed only one short motet, most of his music, especially his powerful organ works, are imbued with his Catholic sensibility.

Chant returned as a major influence, but in spite of Papal support at the start of the century, the second Vatican Council saw the demise of chant and a general deterioration of the musical quality in Roman Catholic worship. In the cathedrals, collegiate chapels and many parish churches in the Anglican Community, the tradition of fine choral singing thrives. Against a background of falling church attendance, congregations at cathedral services, especially Evensong, have been growing, thanks in part to the many excellent recordings of the choral repertoire.

The experience of being a chorister remains the finest musical education a child could have – many of the most renowned singers of today started their singing lives in cathedral choirstalls.

Edward Elgar 1857–1934

Edward Elgar was largely self-taught, spending his early years in Worcester working in his father's music shop, playing the organ, bassoon and violin, conducting and teaching. He visited Paris and Leipzig in his twenties but could not afford to study at the Leipzig Conservatory. His early compositions met with little success but the *Enigma Variations* and *The Dream of Gerontius* made him internationally famous. He lived in London for periods, was knighted and moved in Court circles, but always felt himself to be an outsider. The reputation of his music as representing British Imperial glory belied an insecurity, due to his humble and Roman Catholic origins and lack of formal musical training. His main influences were from the German Romantics, particularly Schumann, and from the Anglican music he heard in Worcester Cathedral. He was the first composer to take the gramophone seriously and recorded much of his music. Following the death of his wife, he returned to Worcester in 1923 and composed little further music. There was a revival of interest in Elgar at the end of his life. The BBC organised a Festival of his music to celebrate his seventy-fifth birthday in 1932 and the following year he flew to Paris to conduct his Violin Concerto with Yehudi Menuhin.

The leaves of the tree were for the healing of the nations (detail), Wilhelmina Geddes, *c.* 1920, stained glass window, St John's Church, Malone Road, Belfast. Image © Artist's Estate. Photograph: Jozef Voda.

The Angel of Peace and Hope, Harry Clarke, 1919, stained glass window, Holy Trinity Church,
Killiney, Co. Dublin. Image © Artist's Estate. Photograph: Jozef Voda.

Mainie Jellett,
Abstact Composition,
c. 1935, oil on canvas.
Image © Crawford
Art Gallery Cork.

The Nativity, Evie Hone,
stained glass window,
1945. Image by kind
permission of *Manresa*,
the Jesuit Centre
of Spirituality,
Dollymount, Dublin.
Image © Artist's Estate.

Ave Maria *– Hail, Mary, full of grace, the Lord is with thee.*
This setting was written in 1887 for the choir of St. George's Catholic Church, where Elgar was assistant organist to his father.
The Choir of Westminster Abbey – James O'Donnell.

Ralph Vaughan Williams 1872–1958

Ralph Vaughan Williams studied at the Royal College of Music in London and at Cambridge University, with Charles Villiers Stanford and Hubert Parry. He then had further lessons with Bruch in Berlin and Ravel in Paris. He began collecting folksongs in 1903 and they remained an influence throughout his long composing life. In 1906 he became the editor of *The English Hymnal*. In the many fine arrangements and new hymns under his name in the first publication of 1906, his interest in both folksongs and the English music of the Tudor period is evident. His wife described him as 'an atheist who later drifted into cheerful agnosticism'. In spite of this, many of the hymns, motets, carols and the *Mass in G* from 1921, dedicated to his friend, Gustav Holst, have a strong devotional feel. *Fantasia on a Theme by Thomas Tallis* is his most popular orchestral work – from 1910. His nine symphonies express a wide range of feelings, often bleak, but also humorous and dramatic.

TRACK 17 – Vaughan Williams

Come Down, O Love Divine *– from* The English Hymnal.
This is one of the most beautiful of the composer's many hymns. The words are by the 14th century Tuscan mystic, Bianco da Siena, and the tune, *Down Ampney*, is named after the Cotswold village where Vaughan Williams was born.
The Choir of Wells Cathedral – Malcolm Archer.

Francis Poulenc 1899–1963

Born in Paris to a wealthy literary and musical family, Francis Poulenc was one of the greatest 20th-century composers for the voice, both in his many song cycles and, from the mid 1930s, in a flow of sacred choral works. Sometimes exuberant, sometimes devotional, and always tuneful, his music is characterised by bittersweet harmonies. He was a member of *Les Six*, a group of young French and Swiss composers associated with Jean Cocteau and other figures of the vibrant cultural life of Paris. He also composed music for the stage, for the ballet – with Diaghilev – chamber music and some popular concertos. He was a fine pianist giving recitals with the baritone, Pierre Bernac, for many years. He was a troubled spirit, experiencing bouts of depression and was deeply affected by the death of a number of close friends.

TRACK 18 – Poulenc

Quem Vidistis – *Who did you see, Shepherds? Speak and tell us.*
From *Quatre Motets pour le Temps de Noël.* First the boys then the men ask the Shepherds – 'what did you see?' Poulenc adds urgency with an emphatic 'Dicite' – tell us! These four motets and another four for the *Time of Penitence* are masterpieces of mid 20th-century choral writing.
The Choir of Westminster Abbey – James O'Donnell.

Benjamin Britten 1913–1976

Although the music of the Far East and of Stravinsky, Mahler and Henry Purcell were important influences, Benjamin Britten's compositions have a strong personal character. After some years in America and London, he moved to Aldeburgh in Suffolk in 1942, where he lived with his partner, the tenor Peter Pears, for the rest of his life, founding the renowned music festival there in 1948. He composed prolifically from childhood and two of his most popular choral works, *A Boy Was Born* and *Hymn to the Virgin,* were written in his teens. It was the opera *Peter Grimes* which brought him to fame in 1945 and his twelve operas mark him as the greatest 20th-century composer of the genre. He was a committed pacifist and refused a knighthood. Though not a churchgoer, his Christian upbringing left a strong spiritual influence on many of his compositions including his *War Requiem* of 1961, his three Church Parables, a Missa Brevis, anthems and cantatas.

TRACK 19 – Britten

That Yongë Child and **This Little Babe so few days old**
from *The Ceremony of Carols.*
This cycle of medieval and 16th-century poems for boys' voices and harp from 1942 remains one of the most popular Christmas works. The poignant *That Yongë Child* is sung by treble Robert Ogden and *This Little Babe* with its canonic excitement must be the greatest tour de force for boys' voices.
The Choir of Westminster Cathedral – David Hill.

John Tavener *b.*1944

London born, John Tavener studied at the Royal Academy of Music intending to become a concert pianist. In the mid 1960s he came to prominence with the cantata, *The Whale* and *The Celtic Requiem* which were recorded by the Beatles' Apple record label. In 1969, he became Professor of Composition at Trinity College, London and Benjamin Britten invited him to write a full length opera for the Royal Opera House, Covent Garden. He was organist at St. John's Presbyterian Church, Knightsbridge, for over fifteen years but in 1977 converted to the Orthodox Church. Most of his compositions are influenced by a strong Orthodox spiritual sense with chant and bells often playing a central role, though In later years his interest has extended to include Eastern religions. In 1989, *The Protecting Veil*, a work for cello and strings, became a huge popular success. He has suffered ill health throughout his life, having had a stroke in his thirties and a heart attack and a tumour in his forties and, since 2007, has been unable to compose.

The Lamb

This simple yet subtle setting of William Blake's poem has become one of the best loved contemporary carols with its contrasting unison, two-part and full choir lines and some delicious dissonances.

The Choir of Westminster Cathedral – James O'Donnell.

Arvo Pärt *b.*1935

Arvo Pärt worked as a sound producer with Estonian radio for ten years. His early compositions were influenced by Russian composers such as Shostakovich and Prokofiev and in 1962 he won a prize for a children's cantata and an oratorio. After a period of experimentation with serialism and twelve-tone composition, which met with disapproval from the Soviet authorities, he began to develop the mesmeric minimalist techniques which have earned him international fame. A major influence was also plain chant and the music of the Orthodox Church. During the 1980s he has also set wider Christian texts, including a *St. John Passion*, a *Te Deum*, *Magnificat* and *Psalms*. In 1980 he moved to live in Berlin. Since 1984 the popularity of his intense ritualistic style, often unadorned and direct, has been helped by a flow of recordings on the ECM record label with the Hilliard Ensemble and Estonian Philharmonic Chamber Choir. In 2008 he composed his first symphony for thirty-seven years, his fourth, named *Los Angeles.*

TRACK 21– Pärt

O Morgenstern – *O Morning star, Gleam of immutable Light*

Magnificat 'O' Antiphon for 21st December.

These Advent chants originated in 8th-century France. The seven prayers were said before and after the Magnificat at Vespers in the week before Christmas – all beginning with the vocative 'O' – a call to God to come to earth to save mankind. Pärt's rich settings were written in 1988 after the composer had moved to Berlin.

Polyphony – Stephen Layton.

Elizabeth Rivers, 'Nativity scene' from *Singing Stars*, 1959,
wood engraving, private collection. Image © Artist's Estate.

God pitched his tent among Men, Patrick Pye R.H.A., 1998,
oil on copper. Image © Patrick Pye.

Hughie O'Donoghue, *Bellacorick* (*Mouth of the Turning River*).
Oil on linen canvas, 175 x 242 cms, 2001. Image © Hughie O'Donoghue.

GLOSSARY OF TERMS

ANTHEM: See Motet.

ANTIPHON: A short chant usually sung before and after a Psalm.

CANTATA: From the Latin – sung (as opposed to *Sonata* – played). A work for one or more voices with instrumental accompaniment. Cantatas were popular as part of Lutheran worship from the 16th century.

CANTUS FIRMUS: A melody, often from chant, used as the musical basis of a Mass or Motet.

CECILIAN MOVEMENT: A 19th-century movement dedicated to restoring chant and early polyphony to the Roman Catholic liturgy.

CONTINUO: Short for *Basso Continuo* – the continuous bass line and sketched in harmonies which underpin all compositions of the Baroque period. It was usually elaborated on a keyboard or other chordal instrument.

LADY MASS: A Mass in honour of the Blessed Virgin Mary, particularly popular in England.

MONASTIC OFFICES/HOURS: The six monastic services of prayer linked to the Psalms. Often all 150 Psalms were sung in a week.
MATINS: Morning – before daybreak.
LAUDS: Praises – at dawn.
PRIME: At the first hour – 6am.
TERCE: At the third hour – 9am.
SEXT: At the sixth hour – midday.

NONE: At the ninth hour – 3pm.
VESPERS: Evening – about 6pm.
COMPLINE: Completion – at the end of the day.
The Anglican Church Offices are
MATINS – or Morning Prayer and
EVENSONG – or Evening Prayer.

MOTET: In medieval times any musical work of two or more parts usually based on a previous melody – often a part of a chant. Later it came to mean any sacred work, usually unaccompanied. The expression ANTHEM was used in the Anglican Church.

ORATORIO: Religious equivalent of opera, though unstaged, often on Biblical subjects with solo singers representing characters. It originated in the Oratories of Rome in the late 16th century. Oratorios played a central role – usually performed by large numbers of musicians – in 19th-century England and Germany.

ORDINARY: The unchanging sections of the Mass.
KYRIE: Have Mercy (Greek).
GLORIA: Glory be to God.
CREDO: I Believe in one God.
SANCTUS: Holy, Holy, Holy.
BENEDICTUS: Blessed is he who comes in the name of the Lord,
AGNUS DEI: Lamb of God.

PARODY MASS: A setting of the Mass using as its musical basis an existing, often secular, song.

POLYPHONY: Literally 'many sounding' – music of more than one part.

PROPERS: The sections of the Mass which vary according to the Feastday.
INTROIT: At the start of Mass.
GRADUAL: After the reading of the Epistle.
ALLELUIA: Before the Gospel.
OFFERTORY: At the presentation of the Bread and Wine and
COMMUNION:
After Communion.

REQUIEM: A Mass for the Dead (*Missa Pro Defunctis*) – from the first word of the Introit 'Requiem aeternam dona eis Domine', (Grant them eternal rest, O Lord).

RESPOND, RESPONSORY: A chant, or polyphonic work, w here a solo voice alternates with a choral refrain.

SEQUENCE: A type of long chant, often of a number of verses to the same melody, popular to around 1150.

TENEBRAE: The Matins and Lauds services of the Wednesday, Thursday and Friday of Holy Week. Candles are traditionally extinguished during the singing of the Psalms until Psalm 51, the *Miserere*, is sung in darkness to symbolise the death of Christ.

TROPE: Words and/or music added to an existing chant.

PUBLISHER ACKNOWLEDGEMENTS

Our thanks to the many friends and colleagues who have helped us to create this book. We are grateful to Tim and Anne Thurston, Aodán Ó Dubhghaill and all the team in RTÉ lyric fm for their unwavering enthusiasm for this project, including Julie Knight, Áine Fay and Eoin Brady. For commenting on the many drafts and suggestions on fine art thanks to Dr Nicola Gordon Bowe, Dr Peter Harbison and Edward Taylor.

We particularly want to thank the staff of the many national collections for their kindness and help in the preparation of this book. Dr Bernard Meehan, Dr Charles Benson and Anne-Marie Diffley of Trinity College Dublin; the Board of Trinity College Dublin; Dr Hugh Maguire and Naomi O'Nolan of the Hunt Museum, Limerick; Glenstal Abbey, Limerick; Fr Paddy Carberry of Manresa House, Dollymount; Fr Donal Neary of St Francis Xavier's Church, Dublin; the National Library of Ireland; the Irish Architectural Archive; the Chester Beatty Library; Waterford Museum of Treasures; the photographic Department of the Department of Arts, Heritage and the Gaeltacht; the Bodleian Library, Oxford; the National Gallery of Ireland; the Crawford Art Gallery, Cork, University College Dublin, University College Cork; the National Museums of Northern Ireland; St. John's Church, Malone Road, Belfast; Holy Trinity Church, Killiney, Co. Dublin; Hyperion Records and Trend Studios.

We would also like to thank Imogen Stuart, Noreen and Patrick Pye, Hughie and Clare O'Donoghue, Oliver Sears, Paddy Bowe, Karen Reihill, David Britton, Josef Vada, Michael Diggin, Evan Salholm, Robert South and Robert Towers. Very special thanks to Kitty Chan for her wonderful pen portraits.

First published in Ireland in 2011 by Associated Editions Limited
33 Melrose Avenue, Fairview, Dublin 3
www.associatededitions.ie

ISBN: 978 1 906429 18 8

Publishing Directors: Anne Brady & Éamonn Hurley
Publishing Co-ordinator: Aoife Kavanagh
Art Editor: Anne Brady
Editorial Assistant: Lily Power
Art Advisors: Dr Nicola Gordon Bowe
 and Dr Peter Harbison
Illustrator: Kitty Chan
Designed by Vermillion Design, Dublin
Printed by Nicholson & Bass

www.rte.ie/lyricfm/gloria
www.hyperion-records.co.uk